there is no moon at my house

PARENTING ADVICE
FROM A VETERAN SCHOOL TEACHER

there is no moon at my house

PARENTING ADVICE
FROM A VETERAN SCHOOL TEACHER

JANICE M. RIALS

Tandem Light Press
950 Herrington Rd.
Suite C128
Lawrenceville, GA 30044

Copyright © 2017 by Janice Rials

All rights reserved. No part of this book may be reproduced, scanned, or transmitted in any printed, electronic, mechanical, including photocopying, recording, or any information storage and retrieval system, without permission in writing from the publisher. Please do not participate in or encourage piracy of copyrighted materials in violation of the author's rights.

Tandem Light Press paperback edition October 2017

ISBN: 978-0-9992633-5-8
Library of Congress Control Number: 2018934198

PRINTED IN THE UNITED STATES OF AMERICA

To my wonderful parents, Theophus and Bernice who loved their children enough to set boundaries.

In loving memory of our oldest brother,
James A. Rials; our gift from God.

"You don't choose your family. They are God's gift to you, as you are to them."

– Desmond TuTu

Contents

Acknowledgments..............................xiii

Introduction................................. xv

Part 1: Bundles of Joy 1

Part 2 : School Days 7

Part 3: Labels as Bandages...................... 19

Part 4 : Giving Your PARENTING POWER Away . . 27

Part 5: Getting Your Power Back................. 33

About the Author 47

Acknowledgments

Thank you to:

GOD for your wisdom,

my daughter for listening,

my family for awesome stories to share,

Genevieve and Dr. Jones for your support and hours of proofreading without complaining, my 750+ students and families that trusted me to make a difference in their lives, and, finally, Tandem Light Press for making my vision come to life.

Introduction

"Lord, help me!" "Have you lost your mind?" Every parent has or will utter these words at some time either in their head or out loud.

Children have not changed—it is the adult's expectations of them that have changed. It is my hope that this book is able to get us thinking about our children. You may think you have a little monster that has taken over the sweet child you gave birth to. How did this happen? How can you fix it?

This book and its contents are not for any certain race or economical group. As an educator and because God has blessed me with the chance to teach in various diverse schools over a thirty-year period, I can truthfully state that what is spoken within this book has no boundaries. Situations occur regardless of your race, culture, and economic background. It is my opinion that there are plenty of people who have done a great job of getting us to think about our spirit and self-worth as well as our relationship with our spouses, but no where do we talk about our children and the affect we have on them.

Over the years, I have learned that children are the same no matter where they are and are seeking the same single thing: *love* and *a safe place to land*! Are you willing to be that parent?

"Kids who need the most LOVE will ask for it in the most UNLOVING ways."

– Author Unknown

Part 1

BUNDLES OF JOY

"Parents are teachers, and home is a child's first and most important classroom."

– Hillary Clinton

When children are born, the birthing process interrupts their safe haven. With a firm hand, the doctor gives them a swat on the butt to take their first breath. This is their first cry for your love and protection as they enter this big, strange place. You are there to give them a loving hug and a smile that says even though the world may swat you I am here holding you tight and to reassure you that everything will be okay.

Most parents do a wonderful job at this stage. You feed them the healthiest foods. You clothe them while making sure that everything that touches their delicate skin is soft and comforting. You go out and purchase special detergent and fabric softeners that you dare not use on anything else. Last but not least, you hold them oh so close and are on-call for every cry. You just can't get enough of that sweet new baby smell. You stand and look at your darling baby as he or she sleeps. You find yourself overcome with excitement as they master each milestone: discovering their little fingers and toes, rolling over for the first time, teething, crawling and then taking that first step. Oh, it is the most wonderful feeling in the world and you would not trade this time for anything.

You do this with great pride and joy and your child knows they are the most precious thing to you. Now let's fast forward to those darling toddler years. It is, in my opinion that in this stage of a child's life, God knew to make children soooo very cute. If he had not done so you would not be able to survive this stage as a parent. This is the stage in a child's life when they start to explore the world or as elders would say, test the waters. We call this the water test. Children in particular have a natural curiosity with water. Before you know it, they'll be standing there, soaking wet from head to toe. This is how every challenge you are faced with starts and your response determines the outcome. For those of you that are wondering what is the water test? It can look like this…

Think back to how many trips you make to that bedroom door with your heart in your hand because you just heard the loudest death wrenching scream only to be told:

"I need a drink of water," "I need to go to the bathroom!" even though they just went. Or the one that works so very well: "I need a hug," for the fifth time when you put your dear child down for a nap or bedtime. This is what I refer to as the early stage of the water test. I am sad to say if you are standing and staring at a child that has been taken over by a monster from ages two to five then you have possibly failed the water test. Let's see how this could have come to be.

About 98 percent of what toddlers do at this stage is truly cute—be it the first time they walk, the sound of their voice and laughter, those loving hugs and kisses—it's the other two percent that concerns me. At this point you begin to wonder what happened to that baby that would just ask for things they really needed like food, a clean diaper, or sleep. As time goes on you notice every time you said either "no" or "stop," your child continued to do whatever they were doing: throwing a tantrum, touching something they should not, hitting, or screaming.

Instead, they just looked back at you or responded with what people like to think of as cute at this stage, "NO!" or "YOU STOP IT" to see if you really meant what you said. Some children will do it again (testing the water) to see just how you will react. Your actions will tell them one of two things: 1) you will always be there to tell me to stop when I need it, or 2) you will think this is cute because I smiled (with my cute little self) and I have the power. Children are so much smarter at this stage than parents seem to think. They learn from your reaction to everything they do. I must warn you, parents, to watch closely at this stage because what is cute at two or four will not be cute later on. Oh yeah, you'll be faced with the same test later, it will just be bigger. Remember, even at this stage, if you find yourself leaving a place because your child is telling you they are ready to go, or you are embarrassed that they are now throwing a tantrum in the middle of the mall, and now you are buying, bribing, or paying your child to behave, you have failed the water test and slowly giving your parenting power to your child. We'll talk more about the power struggle more in a few pages.

Let's be clear, though: I am not in any way suggesting that you must spend every minute, or waking hour with your radar on looking for the water test. Discipline is ongoing, but it must be tempered with love, parental involvement, and lots of special moments; not waiting until a negative behavior becomes an issue causing you or your child to go too far. Take, for instance, the rattle tossing game. Baby or toddler throws the rattle down and you pick it up for them. Let's say you picked it up one, maybe two times, but at the third or fourth time you need to tell them no and then redirect your child in a positive way, which could be as simple as changing their location, activity, or any other positive redirection. With this, you have established that you are aware that they need your attention and that you are here and in control. This is no different than a teacher in the classroom. A child is able to gain control of the class by being the class clown, throwing or writing notes, talking, or whatever they can think of to gain attention. If the teacher does not either redirect the entire class' attention or the disruptive student, it will only get worse every passing minute, hour, or day because that student has taken the teacher's power away. Teachers on an average maintain control and provide a wonderful place for learning for as many as thirty-five students in a classroom.

Now, you, as the parent have had charge of this darling child for five years and it does not matter if you have passed all of the water tests or not, you must now take your handy work to school.

Part 2

SCHOOL DAYS

"Education is a shared commitment between dedicated teachers, motivated students and enthusiastic parents with high expectations."

– Bob Beauprez

Alright, it's the first day of school. Everyone is excited, you have bathed and dressed your child and made sure that they look their very best as you get ready to take that first day of school photo. Through teary eyes, you walk proudly into the school doors to hand over your five years of handy work. As a parent, you need to stop and think about what you have brought that teacher to work with. Keep in mind that you have had five years to teach your child how to treat others with respect, kindness, compassion, and fairness. Once again, I must say that 95 percent of the parents will do this and bring some wonderful children to school; it's the other 5 percent that concerns me. Therefore, let's talk about those 5 percent.

Those parents will proudly walk through the halls with their handy work in tow and present and inform the teacher that…

1. OH, THEY ARE JUST LIKE ME
   Have you ever made this statement? You would not believe how many parents come to school at the beginning of the year or for parent conferences and say with great pride "Oh, they are just like me!" So, you're telling me that you go to work and crawl around on the office floor, shout out, do no work, throw pencils, paper, urinate on the bathroom walls and floor, call your coworkers and boss names other than their birth name, steal from your coworkers, disregard your boss when they ask you to do your job etc.? If so you need to STOP IT! This isn't behavior you would want to see in your workplace or in your child's classroom. I know there is not a parent anywhere that would allow their children to act this way at their place of employment. So, my question is why is it okay that your child can come to school and act this way. Teachers in every economic area have this same issue. During the 45–60 minutes of teaching time, 50 percent of that time is spent handling discipline issues that you could have

addressed long before your child was brought to school. As a parent, you must look at what you are taking pride in. Is this the behavior you want to end up paying for the rest of your life? This is not a child that has boundaries or respect; this is a child that has been given no boundaries and you have given your power as a parent away.

Parents, I would hope that the aforementioned qualities are not the ones you want your child to display as your family legacy. Children must know that their behavior is a reflection of their family because they are part of you. Children, as well as adults associated with any team or organization—be it a baseball team, football team, educators, girl scout, boy scouts etc.—are required to represent them in a positive manner. Therefore, why are you not holding your child responsible for his or her actions and how they represent their family? The most important team children are a part of should be their family.

Another type of child that parents proudly bring to school are…

2. MIRACLE BABIES

As a mother, grandmother, aunt and teacher, I really understand how every parent feels that their child is a miracle. They truly are; however, there are some parents that seem to think they are the only family in the entire world that has been blessed with a miracle child. This child, in their parent's mind, should be handled with kid gloves. This parent will tell you in no uncertain terms that you, as a teacher, and no one else should not and will not hold this child to the same expectations as other children.

To this parent, I have a news flash: all children that are born are miracles from God! He has blessed you as well as millions of others with this little miracle and has commissioned you to be their parent. You are to guide and love them. This means that it is your job to raise them, set boundaries and discipline with a loving touch as God does with us! Think about this: if God gave us everything we wanted, boy, would we be a mess! So, what makes you think it is okay to have a child and not have boundaries? That child that you have allowed to just do and say whatever they want will someday enter some poor teacher's classroom and disrupt another little miracle's education because he/she has no boundaries or respect for themselves or others. Now, is it fair that your miracle grows up thinking that they are the only miracles on God's Green Earth? Is it not fair to say that every one of God's miracles deserve the right to come to school and get an uninterrupted education? How would you feel if your child came home every night stressed out because another child has demanded the teacher's attention all day, or your child had to sit by this child that has been placed everywhere possible in the classroom? That's why this Miracle Baby's behavior will often show up later in life as, "entitlement," which we'll address later.

Now, we have the He's Just Like Me Child, the Miracle Baby and then enter the proud parent that truly believes that…

3. MY CHILD WOULD NEVER LIE TO ME!
Listen parents; as you utter those words to yourselves or form your mouth to say it out loud you know it is human nature to lie. There are times when you have been faced with things you do not want to accept when confronted and you, too, will lie. So why do you think children will not do the same. As humans, we lie for several reasons. The lies that show up early in children's behavior are to help avoid punishment, escape accountability, or to get things that are not theirs. It is safe to say that lying does not just start when they come to school, as most parents want teachers to believe.

By the way, let's just call it what it is. It is not a little white anything, it is not a story— these terms send the wrong message to children. They read stories in school and reading is a good thing. There is absolutely nothing good about lying, so call it what it is so children will understand the difference. Let's look at how a child becomes skilled at lying.

How many times has your child heard you tell

some of those stories adults like to call just Little White Lies? Everyone may have told a few of these because you didn't want to hurt someone's feelings, and don't forget all those "the one that got away" stories that seem to be so exaggerated you can hardly believe it yourself (I'm guessing to make it sound better to those listening). Or, you may have done the following: Let's say Little J misses school one day, on the next day you send in a note and it states: "Little J was ill." The teacher reads it and then says, "I am so glad you feel better." Little J turns and replies, "I wasn't sick," then goes on to tell the teacher some of the following reasons for their absence: we went to the baseball game, my parent over slept and said we can just sleep in, or, my clothes weren't clean, I couldn't find my shoes, we had a party, we were out of town and got in late. You would be surprised at some of the real reasons children miss school. Another excuse, or little white lie, I've heard reminds me of the inspiration for the book title: There is No Moon at My House.

Homework seems to bring out the art of lying in some parents and children. I thought I had heard and read all the excuses, as parents like to call it when in fact sometimes it is just a lie. There was the, I-am-not-doing-homework-with-my-child-because-"I Have a Life" parent, the "My child is failing and all this homework is not necessary" parent, "We did not have a pencil to complete the work" parent (as they write the note in pencil), the "you are expecting way too much of my miracle baby" parent, just to share a few. The one that tops all of them was a note a parent wrote on a month-long project. The assignment was to look up at the moon every evening and record just ten changes of moon phases over a period of one month. The child proudly returned their homework with the following note written across the recording sheet, "My child could not do this homework because there was no moon at my house." *There was no moon at my house.* Now, I am well aware that this could possibly be true, there are some areas that it is difficult to see the moon at times, but let me tell you, some children will gladly share with their teachers exactly what happened. As the project was handed in I was told that they did not want to do this project and the parent said it was okay. What a lesson you just taught your child. Not only is it just fine to not be responsible, it is just fine to lie about it also. It is no wonder children are such masters at lying now at such a young age; they have learned from the pros. They are so good at it that lying comes in various forms from children.

So these are some of the creative fabrications I've heard from that five percent I spoke of earlier over the last thirty years of teaching…

"I Found It"

We have all heard this and some of us have even used it in our younger days. This reminds me of when I was coming up. My mother did not believe in finding anything! And I do mean anything, no matter what it was. We were raised that if you or your parents did not buy it for us it did not belong to you; therefore, you did not lose it for it to be found. I remember my brother bringing home a chain from a tow truck and told my mother he found it. Now, I have no idea what he planned to do with it, but I promise you it was not the same thing my mother had in mind for him to do with it. She took that chain and wrapped it around him and told him to walk around the block. She placed me in the bay window of the third-floor apartment and I had to count his three trips around the block. Then he had to walk back to the exact place he found it and put it back. Please don't try this now because you will be on video so fast and more than likely arrested. Needless to say, he never did that again and we learned from his mistake, so much so that one day when we were older we were walking to school and we saw a pencil on the ground. One brother was tempted to pick it up and then it hit him that if he brought that pencil in the house he was going to have to explain to mom that he found it. Well, that pencil may still be on the ground today or someone else took it, but it did not go home with us! See, if you "nip it in the bud" (take care of issues when they first occur) as my mom use to say, you will not be faced with, "I found it!" being a phone call saying please come to the police department to pick your child up for stealing. You must keep in mind if a child is allowed to come home with an item from school and tell you they found it and you allow them to keep it, that little brain is thinking: *Wow! That lie works and I didn't get in trouble.* You get the picture.

The next type of child is the mystery child named…

"I Don't Know"

This is the mystery child that every parent has unknowingly given birth to. This poor child has been blamed for almost everything that has ever happened. No matter what you ask your child their answer is "I don't know." This mystery child will soon take over your dear child to the point that all they can do is hunch their shoulders and give you that surprised look on their face that seems to say: "I can't believe you are asking me what happened." If we could ever find I Don't Know, he or she will have lots to answer for.

Some of us have children that would make awesome…

"Lawyers"

The Lawyer child has figured out that if they can cast a shadow of doubt on themselves by blaming someone else- a sibling, friend, parent, teacher, pet or anybody or anything other than themselves. It is sad to say that this is one tactic that seems to work very well when they start school. This starts very early in a child's life especially if they have a younger or older sibling that seems to test the water more than the one that is lying. This happens in school quite a bit. The student in the class that has behavior issues—you know them; we spoke of them earlier, Miracle Baby and Just Like Me children—seems to get blamed for everything in the class and most teachers are aware of this, but that child will go home and tell his/her parents it wasn't their fault but another child's fault. Wow! Another one that works. Now we get to the dear sweet child that plays…

"To Tell The Truth, But…"

This is when the child starts out telling you the truth then quickly shifts the blame. It sounds like this: "Did you take the Pokémon cards off the teacher's desk?"

Child answers slowly, "Yeeeaaah," and in the same breath throws in the "but… _____told me to," or "_____ did it first," and the one I have heard for years: "_____ made me do it." It is amazing that we do not hold our children responsible for their actions. Children must be held accountable for their actions. I have yet to meet a teacher that has so much time on their hand that they have nothing else to do but make up things to tell you your child did. As a teacher, I cannot tell you how many times I sent notes home after many warnings and the parent's response was, "Well, he said he didn't do it," or "It was another child's fault." Parents, I can assure you that if your child's teacher has sent you a note, nine times out of ten it is because your child was responsible for the action.

As I have said over and over again, children are like sponges and they take in everything you do because you are the role model.

Don't worry that children never listen to you; worry that they are always watching you.

> \- Robert Fulghum

Part 3

LABELS AS BANDAGES

"The way we talk to our children becomes their inner voice."

– Peggy O'Mara

As adults, we play such an important role in children's lives. It is a role that is not easy, very time consuming and one that you cannot be selfish about. There are times we need to step back and assess our role in our children's progress. Often it is easier to put labels on children than it is to deal with what is really true. Let's talk about a few of these more common labels and why they exist.

Mean Children

I have had several adults tell me that some children are just born mean. This is so far from the truth. Think about this: why would God who is *love* do such a thing? With that said, I know you have noticed children that just always seem to have a frown on their face, and ready to fight anyone that looks their way and thought to yourself, "Boy, kids are just mean or mad with the world." Well some of them are, but let's just look at who is their world. Over a child's lifetime they will have lots of adults with whom they come in contact, be it teachers, coaches, church members, neighbors, family members and a host of others and the most important adults, their parents. Sadly, all of these adults will let them down at some point. You can let children down in many ways, but the one that causes their frown and anger is a lack of love that reassures a child that: they are loved, they can count on you, you are their safe haven, you've got their back. You know the love we spoke of earlier? The love you showed your child when they were first born?

Society wants us to believe that to show love is how much you give in material things. The feeling that you must work hard to give them the designer clothes, a fancy house, the ability to go out and eat at the best restaurants, buy the latest high tech item, the latest high dollar gym shoes, get nails and hair weave done every week, new cars and so on. Parents, you are not the only ones that let children down, but you are the most powerful one in this situation because children love their parents and look to you to give them support and unconditional love, Not just material things.

Here's the letdown: the child loses in the end. Believe it or not you have never seen a child looking for any of those things when they are born, feeling down, or sick. What a child would really rather have is a hug from you, beans and cornbread at a table with their family. They would love to know that parents will take the time out of their busy day to toss a ball, shoot some hoops, or ride a bike with them. You know, the types of things years later when they are all sitting around with family and friends talking about their childhood memories seem to always bring a smile to their face. Not one of my childhood stories has ever been about the time I had a pair of designer jeans or my house had six bedrooms. Hold on. Before you get bent out of shape, it started out with three and then the attic was converted into three more, but I can tell you about how my dad took the time to build it with the help of four children. Memories. I can tell you about a mom that would bake your favorite cake on your birthday then let you lick the spoon and the bowl afterward, go to the ends of the earth for you, go on bike rides with you and meant what she said. I can also tell you about a dad who watched Saturday morning cartoons with us, tossed a ball around, sped down a dirt road going back to his homestead, played with his children, set boundaries and gave and stuck to his word. These are the things that a child longs for.

Memories like these are what make a child have that

loving smile on their face, not how much money and *things* we have. All the material things are most often what the adult wants because to an adult it is all about what we have to show the world. Think about the times that people had thirteen or more children and raised them up to be model citizens and have become doctors, lawyers, teachers etc. Sometimes not knowing or not caring that they were what society considered as poor because what they were given was more precious than any material thing they could have gotten. Love, self-worth, and respect outweighs anything else. Now, understand I am not saying shame on you if you are able to provide a better life for your child, I am saying just don't let it get in the way of what's really important and please don't sacrifice your child for any of it. Be their hero!

Entitled

Entitlement is the latest bandage label we have for our children. Let's examine the definition of entitlement. According to Google search: entitlement is 1. the fact of having a right to something 2. the amount to which a person has a right 3. The belief that one is inherently deserving of privileges or special treatment. How could our dear sweet children come to have this label placed on them. One suggestion is that we must look at how adults around them respond to their demands, and wants. It can look like this…

If you are at your child's elementary graduation and have just handed him or her a top of the line brand new iPhone but you know he or she has done nothing to earn it. You have been called to the school so many times and made more excuses for their various behavior problems, write ups, failing grades and lies over the six years of his or her elementary education. You, my dear, are doing a wonderful job of creating an entitled child. This child has no reason to respect anything or anyone—including you. They value nothing. They have no motivation, which will really be ugly and costly to you, as they get older. This behavior shows up no matter where you are.

These Entitlement children truly believe that they are inherently deserving of privileges or special treatment. When a child is given the opportunity to earn things it fosters great pride. Not to mention, if they work to earn it they will be more likely to take care of it.

This brings to mind children that are given a brand-new car when they first start to drive. It has been proven that nine times out of ten that they will wreck that car or they will allow someone else to wreck it. Think back on how you felt when you earned your first paycheck, or you saved up to buy that special toy, or a gift for yourself or your parent. It is okay to let children earn what they want. Let them feel pride. I never knew how earning your own things had such an impact on not only you, but others around you until I was putting a book together for my oldest brother. We were raised on the south side of Chicago in Englewood and my brother worked as a busboy (dish washer) for Walgreen's his sophomore year of High School. He saved his money for a year along with paying rent. And, yes, we had to pay rent once you became employed to contribute to the household, which prepared us for the future. He saved every dime he made, rode the bus to and from work and did not buy anything because he was determined to buy his first motorcycle. He purchased a Yamaha 350 once he graduated from high school. He worked and saved again and purchased his first car 1983 Mach 1 Mustang. While putting a birthday book together for his fiftieth, I asked friends and family to write a note to him. I was so surprised how he not only took great pride in his accomplishments, but so did the neighborhood children and family members. Several friends and family members wrote about how they were motivated by him to do the same thing. I bet you can think of several things you worked for and remember how you felt. Why would you rob your child of that same sense of pride?

The worst case of entitlement and loss of power that I have ever witnessed in my life was when I was in a department store and this child, about ten years old, wanted a certain pair of gym shoes. When his mother told him he could not have them, he stood up and punched his mother in her back so hard that she buckled under. She said absolutely nothing to that child. I think it is safe to say that this was either an Entitled or Friend-child early on in life. This mother had lost all of her power as a parent and this behavior did not just start on that day (it was probably cute when he would hit her back as a toddler and as I said, it is not cute when they get older)!

Remember, as a parent you must "Keep the End in

Mind!" Entitled children grow up to be entitled adults. Believe me: the world will give them nothing they do not earn. Therefore, they will feel that it is okay to get it from you or your neighbors because they really do not care who they get it from because they are entitled.

BFF's

Children that are allowed to be their parents *friend* have a hard time with respect and self- control often. This is most often the child that has no regard for adult authority because in their world, there is none; they rank at the same level as their parents. The problem with this child usually does not become an issue until they start school. In class, this is often the student that has no problem talking back to the teacher. *Friend*-children think they run the class and things should go their way. When it doesn't, there is lots of attitude and pouting. They will go home and tell their parents that the teacher does not like them, they don't like school, the teacher is mean—and rightfully so based on that child's prior roles with adults—though the parent usually says that they have never or do not have trouble with their child at home.

Let's look closely at the child/parent role at home. The first thing I need you to notice at home is whether or not you tell or ask this child anything that goes against their *friend* rights, they usually respond with the guilt trip, "You don't like me. You're mean!" These usually work because God forbid that your friend-child does not like you. As friend-children get older, parents then start to share conflicts that they are having with other adults. Friend-children will often take part in or interrupt adult conversations because no one has ever told them that there are adult conversations that they are not privy to. Friend-children often run their house, too. By this I mean they dictate when, where, and what happens daily in their lives. Roles become reversed and blurred. You, as a parent, will find yourself doing whatever it takes to pacify your child, even going into debt just so that your child is not mad at you because you want to remain friends. Friend-children will most often grow into entitlement children.

The only bandage you should ever put on your child should be the temporary ones that come in a little box. If you must label your child let the label read: I Am Loved

Part 4

GIVING YOUR PARENTING POWER AWAY

"No one can just take your power; we can only give it away through our actions."

– J. Rials

I mentioned this power thing when we were talking about your toddler. You probably said to yourself, "Really there is no way children at this age could possibly be playing power games!" Believe it or not, you often give your power away to your children. This shift starts at a very young age. You're probably wondering how this is possible. Well, let's look at when and how this happens.

Playing Both Sides

Have you ever told your child they cannot do or have something and they go ask the other parent, because they did not get the response they wanted from you? For example, your child wants to go to the mall with a group of children that you know are troublemakers, and mom or dad says no. Then the other parent comes home and sees the long face, asks what's wrong, sometimes not realizing that a decision was already made prior to their arrival and allows the child to go. If the first parent does not address this decision, or says nothing because you don't want to fight this battle, and allows your child to go anyway, you and your spouse have now given your power away.

By the way, this example is based on a child that would now be a teenager, but trust me it starts way before that and can happen at any age. By the teen years they are pros at it. Think back to when your toddler wanted something a cookie, candy or a toy and one parent said no and the other said okay. You have found when it really started. Remember: toddlers are little sponges and what you think is no big deal is a learning experience for children.

Choosing Battles

Have you ever found yourself trying to get your children up for school and they take their own sweet time, mumbling and moaning during the process? You know exactly what I'm talking about. When they finally get dressed and into the car you are now late because of their earlier stubbornness. You struggle with this every day and those in denial say to themselves, "choose your battles." For example, you normally stop and pick up breakfast but you notice the time and cannot stop today. When you tell them you are not stopping here comes the pouting, crying, folded arms and all the rest of the craziness you allow and again you say this is not worth the fight. You now feel bad; I don't for the life of me know why. Oh, yes, I do. Because this too is a battle you have chosen not to fight, because you feel like the worst parent in the world. You decide to be late for work to get this pouting, screaming and move "when I feel like it," door-slamming child some breakfast. Look at what this child has learned because it is learned behavior. Remember the water test where I said it was going to get bigger? Well here it is: sitting in the back of your car at the age of ten and above if not younger. I bet it's safe to say that this happens on a daily basis and because you chose not to fight the battle and correct it the first time, children can use their power on a daily basis whenever they don't get what they want.

Disconnected

Our new loss of power has come in the form of technology. Take a day and look around and notice how disconnected we have become as a family. You can see it everywhere you go, at the ballpark, restaurants, parks, on vacations, family cookouts, and riding in the car—you get the message. How many times have you seen this happen? A family comes into a restaurant. There is a mother, father, two children between the ages of nine and eleven, and a grandparent. They all sit down. The parents have their devices out and on before they are seated. Once seated, the children each get on their devices. They look up long enough to order their food and afterward not one of them look up from their device until the food arrives. The grandparent sits there with her entire family and not one of them speak a word to each other. What a missed opportunity to hold conversation, talk about your day, laugh, and share stories and enjoy each other's company. As you see, it is not only the children who are responsible for the growing disconnect between family members. Parents are also guilty because they are wrapped up in their own mobile phones, checking emails or watching TV. What an awesome time that you could spend talking to, playing with, or just listening to your children. Parents often find themselves using devices as babysitters, homework tutors, and entertainment.

Cris Rowan wrote a blog titled, "The Impact of Technology on the Developing Child,"[1] which highlights the impact of technology on developing children. Rowan discusses the finding of a survey conducted by Kaiser Foundation in 2010. He writes "A 2010 Kaiser Foundation study showed that elementary aged children use on average 7.5 hours per day of entertainment technology, 75 percent of these children have TV's in their bedrooms, and 50 percent of North American homes has the TV on all day. Gone are the dining room table conversations, replaced by the "big screen" and take out." The Kaiser Foundation

1 www.huffingtonpost.com/cris-rowan/technology-children-negative-impact_b_3343245.html

shows not only a disconnection in the family comm-unication, it is also having an impact on children's development. The Kaiser study found that there are four critical factors necessary to achieve healthy child development: movement, touch, human connection, and exposure to nature. This research did not include the media we use now. Over a six-year period with all of the new technology children spend as much as nine hours a day, on average, on some form of technology. The disconnections continue to grow with every new game and device that is developed. Technology has aided in our being so very disconnected with each other.

I AM READY TO GO!

Parents can give their power away when they find themselves leaving an event because their child tells them it's time to go, while stating it with authority. When you give no response, you leave the question to be answered by the child, or the world's worst response to something that happens is "I choose the battles I want to fight with my child." Parents might as well tell them to do whatever they want.

Now that you know how you have lost your power and why these behaviors are happening, are you saying, "Lord, how can I get my power back?" Let me tell you, yes, you can! Just read on.

Part 5

GETTING YOUR POWER BACK

"There is no such thing as a perfect PARENT. So just be a REAL one."

– Robert Fulghum

One of my favorite Andy Griffith shows is the episode titled: "Opie and the Spoiled Kid." (1963). A new little kid moves into town that had no regards to following any of the town rules about riding his bike. He continues to run people over on the sidewalks and had to be asked several times to follow the rules. He was very disrespectful and did not feel he had to follow the rules because his dad always defended him. Andy warns the child that the next complaint he would lose his bike.

He then tells Andy that he could tell his daddy and he would make it right. Sounds like a miracle baby? He goes on to tell Opie that he has a new seventy-dollar bike and gets an allowance without having to do chores. Poor Opie thought about this and went to question his dad as to why he had to work for his allowance and he needed a raise. Well, the story goes on with the two boys talking and the little kid tells Opie how to get his way by holding his breath, having a fit and rolling around on the floor. Opie tries it out on Andy, to see if he can get a raise in his allowance from twenty-five cents to seventy-five cents without working for it. Andy handles it (to me) in a classic way. He just asks what he's doing each time in a calm, concerned voice (giving recognition), and tells him to be careful not to get his clothes too dirty (giving loving advice) and then continues to work. Well, Opie saw that this did not work as well for him and when he was all done with his performance Andy gives him what I call a good old…

Because I Said So

A good old "Because I Said So" works wonders. Opie had to do his chores to earn the allowance because Andy said so and those were the rules. I know we let our children have a voice and this is good, just like in the Andy Griffith episode it is great to listen to your child, but you are the adult and know what is best for your children. There are times when there is no room for arguing or negotiating especially if it is going to harm the character of that child in the future. As a child, they will come across situations where they will need to do something because you told them to do it; end of discussion.

As an adult, do you go to your job and negotiate or argue about why you must do the things your job description requires you to do in order to be a productive employee? Have you ever asked your boss why you need to turn your computer on, sharpen your pencils, make a phone call, or eat lunch in 30-60 minutes? Then think about this, are you going to argue, or negotiate, every time you ask your child to do something? I would hope not. Children should be raised to trust that you would not tell them something that requires them to question you or your actions, the same way you trust the company that you work with. Now, when they do question you, and they will, how you handle it will determine if you maintain your parent power.

As a parent, it is okay to tell your child "because I said so." You have the right because you were chosen to raise this child. In case you are wondering how this will affect your child in school, let me share this thought with you. What should the teacher do during an emergency in school and your child is used to you telling them or asking them to do something three or four times before they even decide to recognize that you are even talking to them? Not to mention getting them to do something. What are they to do with the child that has been allowed to move when they get ready or not even after being asked several times? I have had this conversation with students often after trying to get Miracle Baby, and Just Like Me students to line up for a fire drill. "Because I said so" will help that child have undisputed boundaries and respect for adults and you will not as I have said before have given your Parenting Power away.

Mean What You Say

As a parent, we must do this without thinking. I remember when my mom revisited this lesson. My youngest brother was about four or five years old and he was jumping up and down on his bed one day. In our house that was a big NO, NO and all of the older children knew that because we to had tested the water. Some more than the others. Well, he being the youngest one always had to test the water for himself on a daily basis. My mother's response to him jumping on the bed was "Do It One More Time!" Well guess what, he did! Yes, he jumped one more time! We could not believe it because we knew exactly what she meant, just by the tone of her voice, but this daily water tester, in my opinion, had lost his mind. We all knew he was in big trouble and would be sentenced to mopping the floors or washing windows or walls, cleaning the bathroom, sweeping the front porch and then making you sit on it and all you could do is watch your friends as they play. She would also send you to bed so early you just lay there and listen to your friends as they played happily and everyone knew you were in trouble, or just an old-fashioned butt whopping. Yes, my mom had ways to get her point across without ever laying a hand on your butt. She had no problem with whopping your butt and often times we would rather she did the later. By the way, I use to think we had the cleanest walls and house in the neighborhood! When asked why he did it, he replied, "Mom, you told me to do it one more time." I did tell you earlier that children were very smart and always thinking. To my surprise, she could do nothing but laugh and say, "Well, I did tell him to do it just one more time." She knew that we were raised to trust that she meant everything she said and he did just what she said without questioning it. Now soon after the laughter she made it real plain to him, "Don't jump on that bed again," and he knew she was not playing with him. As a parent, you must always mean what you say because your reputation is at stake.

Follow Through

As a parent, you must follow through. If you tell a child that *you are or are not going* to do something they should know that you mean that. I was faced with this once with my daughter and niece. On Saturdays, we would go to the mall and the girls were old enough to walk around the mall together. Well, before they left me they were instructed to meet me at a given time and at a certain spot. I made it very clear that if they were not back at that time I was going to leave and they would have to walk home. (We did not live far from the mall.) Guess what? They didn't show up at the given time and I am not one that believes in waiting on children. The given time came and I left. They had to walk home. The next trip to the mall they were at the meeting spot before I got there. My niece still talks about the time I left them in the mall and that Aunt Janice mean exactly what she says.

I have often heard parents threaten their young children with punishments that are impossible to follow through with. For instance: I am going to ground you for life. Really? If you do this you too will be grounded because you can't leave your child at home forever, not until they are at least eighteen and even then, that is questionable. These threats soon become idol threats and the children know it. Children can wait you out far longer than you can them if this is your strategy.

On the other hand, I have also seen the parent that promises the child everything and has yet to deliver any of it no matter how simple. If you tell a child you are going to play ball, go bike riding, go to the movies, reward them in any way you must keep that promise. If you are not able to keep a promise a child will understand if you are honest and have a good reason, saying nothing or just not doing it because you knew when you said it that it was not going to happen will then cause your child to lose trust in you and they soon start to just hear *blah, blah, blah* when you talk. Therefore, the trust that they have developed for you slowly goes away.

I cannot tell you how many times students have made the statement "My dad (or mom) said they are coming to school," and never come leaving the teacher with a heartbroken child that they now have to comfort. Just like you and your friends trust is something you build and earn and once broken it is very hard to regain. It is the same with children's trust in you as parents and when that trust is broken it to is very hard to regain. As the elders would say "Don't write a check you can't cash!

Reconnect

It has been more than twenty years since children's main source of entertainment was playing outside, playing hide and seek, bike riding, jumping rope, hop scotch, jacks, rock teacher and a good old game of baseball or football just for the fun of it. Even though we cannot argue about how important and necessary it is to incorporate technology into a child's development, it should not take the place of parental involvement. The disconnection that it has caused within and among your family should be a major concern (remember that section in our previous chapter?) It is amazing how many times parents have made the statement that they can't get their children to put their phones or devices away. It is an easy solution: if you are paying the bill or they are living in your house you have the right to tell them to turn it off, now if this does not work then believe it or not you can take possession of them. Find a drawer, mantle, lock box, etc. and put them in it. Now if you feel you can't physically take it, then call the phone company and have it turned off until they understand that you mean what you say. You have that right; remember you are paying the bill! Now you must also lead by example: put your devices away and engage with your children. It is easy to start with little steps because it will be like weaning them off their bottle when they were babies. An hour a day and gradual increases of time is a good start to reconnect and gain your power back.

Get Your Own Friends

Think back to our BFF section in Part 3. Now, as you look over the list of synonyms of what a friend is, nowhere do you see daughter, son, or children.

synonyms: companion · soul mate · intimate · confidante · confidant · familiar · alter ego · second self · playmate · playfellow · classmate · schoolmate · workmate · ally · associate · sister · brother · best friend · kindred spirit · bosom buddy · bosom friend · pal · chum · sidekick · crony · main man · mate · buddy · bud · amigo · compadre · homeboy · homegirl · homie · dawg · gal pal · BF · BFF · peeps · compeer

Many parents want to be their child's friend. God made you older than your child for a reason. You need to think with an adult head and always ahead of your child in order to guide them. Both of you cannot be walking side by side with the same authority on the path of life! Parents have become so involved in their child's social life that they begin to take the role of a peer. Let me tell you what this looks like. Are you phoning your kid's friends, commenting on their Facebook page, involved in their personal conflicts with their friends? You are not your child's friend; you are the parent. Therefore, stand up and be one. God did not put you here to be your child's friend. Get your own friends. Your child needs your guidance, love, and for you to be their safe place to fall and the one they can count on. When you act as a "friend," the lines of authority can become blurred, roles of parent and child often times reverse and the child will develop an air of superiority. We are the only species that want to be friends with our children and still have power as a parent instead of their parent. Being your child's friend is so much easier than being their parent but research has found that kids do better with parents that show affection and enforce age appropriated limits. You may pay a higher price in the end if your 30+year-old friend is still sleeping on your couch in your retirement years.

Keep the End in Mind

As a parent, it is your job to raise your children. A good rule of thumb to keep in mind while doing so is to "Raise Your Children with the End in Mind." Now, hold on and let me explain. I am not saying you need to plan your child's entire life. I am not saying pick a career for them or anything like that. What I am saying is to take a good look at your child's behavior. Now fast forward and then think about what this behavior will look like if it continues. It is not WHO you want your child to be it is WHAT you want them to be: loving, kind, honorable, respectful, and caring. If you raise your child to have these qualities, you will not need to worry about who they will grow up to be.

Family Roots

Roots can grow in many directions as well as close to the plant. How strong and healthy those roots perform will determine how well generations of that plant will survive. How we interact with our children can determine how generations of our offspring will be effected. Let's explore this: A child that grows up in a nurturing, loving, proud family will most often have that same type of family when they grow up. Are you going to be the family that causes the roots to go in a different direction?

Children need to know their family and its history. I often tell my students and grandchildren that when you are out you show the world how much you love your family, as well as what we stand for. Children need to understand that their actions affect more than just them, but their entire family. Everyone needs to feel a sense of belonging, with family pride comes a sense of belonging. Children need to understand that how they act represents their family.

They Don't Come With A Manual

How many times have you heard this statement "I'm doing the best I can," or "they didn't come with a manual"? Well they did not need a manual. God put in place a thing called a family: parents, grandparents, aunts, uncles, and friends. We need to build that village back up because no matter what you think, as the African Proverb states: "It does take a village to raise a child." It seems that everyone has decided to do their own thing and in the mean time we've lost our children and now need a manual. If you find yourself, as a parent over whelmed or just doesn't know what to do in a situation. May I suggest you look around and find that special friend or coworker that has raised their children and ask them. As a teacher, no matter how many years of experience we all go to other teachers for advice and suggestions. It is okay to listen to and get suggestions from other parents and then decide what will work best for you and yours. There are times when we are too close to the situation to even think straight—I know I have had those days. You may find that the situation is not as bad. As the saying goes two heads are sometimes better than one. This is where your village can really help. Just remember, whatever your definition of success entails, one thing for sure is that a strong foundation is an essential piece.

I'd like to leave you with something my aunt wrote about my grandmother and my brother shared about our parents. Hopefully it will help inspire you to think about what you want your children to remember about how you parented them. Do you want them to remember that you were on the phone all the time? That you gave them "things" instead of spending quality time with them? What will your children say about you?

> "The most memorable times were spent with my mom. I admired my mom very much because of her Christianity and how much she loved God.

She often took the time to teach us about God and the Bible. I admire her for raising us to be obedient, intelligent, and not to get with the wrong people. She often said if you hang around smart people, mostly you'll be smart. This lesson could be applied to everything you do in life. My mom was my first educator. She taught me how to read and spell; because of her I am an excellent reader today. I remember how I would call her every morning. I could talk to her about anything—she was mom, my role model. I loved my mom so very much and she is my fondest childhood memory. I thank God for allowing her to be my mom."

– Janice B. age 68

"As I think back, one of many things that stand out about our parents was the confidence in us that they had. I can't remember there ever being a time, situation, event, goal or dream that we were talked out of trying or told we couldn't do or achieve."

– Jerry

"If you are completely exhausted and don't know how you're going to keep giving this much of yourself day after day, you're probably a good parent."

– Bunmi Laditan

Love is not what you say.
Love is what you do!

Author unknown

About the Author

Janice Rials is a native of Chicago, Illinois. She graduated from National College of Education where she earned an AA in Early Childhood Education. She then went on to earn her Bachelors of Science in Education at Bradley University in Peoria, Illinois, and then earned her Masters of Arts in Teaching at Piedmont University of Demorest, Georgia.

Janice has enjoyed a rich and diverse professional life as an educator for more than thirty years. She has served as a pre-K through sixth grade classroom teacher, grade facilitator, and cluster trainer for Gwinnett Teacher Math Institute. Janice is a daughter, a sister, aunt, single mother, grandmother, and most importantly, a teacher to hundreds of elementary school students and their parents. She was awarded Georgia's Race to the Top for outstanding student achievement.

www.ingramcontent.com/pod-product-compliance
Lightning Source LLC
Chambersburg PA
CBHW050447010526
44118CB00013B/1715